This book belongs to

____

____

____

For the best results use coloring pencils to prevent bleed-through on each page.
If using markers then place a blank sheet of paper behind the page you are coloring to prevent the color from running into the next image.

Copyright © 2020 by Darby Yates

ISBN: 9798684281167